LED TO GREEN PASTURES

LED TO
GREEN PASTURES

by
RUTH HAINSWORTH

Published by
ARTHUR JAMES LIMITED
THE DRIFT   EVESHAM   WORCS.
WR11 4NW

First Edition 1977

© Ruth Hainsworth 1977

All rights reserved by the publishers
Arthur James Limited of Evesham, Worcs., England

ISBN 0 85305 192 5

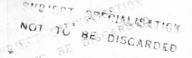
MADE AND PRINTED IN GREAT BRITAIN BY PURNELL AND SONS LTD.,
PAULTON (BRISTOL) AND LONDON

Foreword

By the Rev. George Bennett,
President of the Divine Healing Mission and former
Warden of Crowhurst Home of Healing.

HOMES of Healing have played a significant part in the recovery by the Church of her healing ministry in our day and generation. They have demonstrated in a practical manner the truth of the old text "He is the same, yesterday, to-day and forever" and have shown that where true faith and love abound, Christ heals through His Church as He ever did of old. Such Homes have brought healing and renewal to many thousands.

This is the story, told by its Founder, of one of our leading Homes—Green Pastures, the Home of Health and Healing at Branksome Park, near Bournemouth and Poole. I have known Sister Ruth Hainsworth for many years, and have always been deeply impressed by the way she overcame many obstacles in order to bring Green Pastures into being. Ruth herself would say it is all a matter of simple obedience to the guiding and enabling call and power of the Good Shepherd; and she would—as she does indeed in this story—pay tribute to all who have helped her, but those who know Ruth, and especially the thousands who have stayed at the Home, would agree that it was only her own indomitable faith and courage that brought Green Pastures into being.

She tells of her own experience of Christ's healing touch in her life. Suffering from what in medical terms could only have been called a hopeless condition, following a severe car accident, she was led first to Crowhurst and then to Resthaven. Here, in these Homes, there was born in her that there was something the Good Shepherd wanted her to do. She felt the divine call to found a new Home where, in an atmosphere of Christian rest and peace, sick and troubled folk could find that deeper healing which only Christ can give.

This is the story of those early days at Branksome Park when, through prayer and devotion, her dream became reality. All who know and love Green Pastures will welcome this book, thanking God for the Home of which it speaks, and the knowledge that under the inspired leadership of its new Director, the Rev. William E. Burridge, Green Pastures will be guided into new and yet more glorious paths.

Contents

DEDICATION

With Gratitude
to God

that the late Rev A. D. Belden D.D., the late Griffith Evans, F.R.C.S., M.A., D.M., and Miss Clare Wadley were able to help make the vision a reality.

CHAPTER 1

The Promise of Guidance

I will instruct thee and teach thee in the way in which thou shalt go:
I will counsel thee with Mine Eye upon thee.

Ps. 32.8

"I AM VERY SORRY but you will not be able to work again. Your capacity for walking will also be very limited."

This was the opinion of four different doctors when I was in my mid-thirties.

I had been working for fourteen years with the National Children's Home. My duties as a Deaconess Sister required me to tour large areas of the country. I was very busy and very happy. I felt that I had been guided by God to my work, and expected that I would happily continue it until my retirement. I could even envisage the day when I would be called upon to take my place in an Elderly Workers' Home; but I was soon to discover that God had very different plans for me.

A car was indispensable for the work, and I had had some very old second-hand specimens which served reasonably well till it became possible to buy an Austin Seven, the first new car I had ever had. In this I set out for a lecture tour in Shropshire. The car was travelling well, in spite of a slight wobble—which I diagnosed was caused by a flat tyre. I stopped at a garage and had all the tyres seen to, and I was soon on my way again. I had travelled about two miles when without further warning the car overturned. It was discovered later that it was faulty when it left the factory. A part of the steering had been left unconnected—some unexplained shortcoming by an unknown workman.

I was pinned inside, and it took some hours to release me. When the doctors saw me in hospital they found that I had fractured my spine and skull, and there were other complications. For several years I was in and out of hospitals and nursing homes, years that I scarcely remember. My life consisted of one operation or treatment after another. My head injuries were the most disturbing, as I had the most painful headaches. I could not think clearly and stumbled with double vision. At times I would collapse in a heap on the floor in a coma. It was quite obvious that I could not carry on my work in the Sisterhood of the National Children's Home, and I very reluctantly resigned. I made a partial recovery and later was able to leave the hospitals and nursing homes and return to my parents' home in Leeds. Here I made further progress, but was still plagued with headaches and dizziness. But I was determined to make a fresh start, and when I was offered the General Secretaryship of the National Free Church Women's Council I accepted it. This work was of considerable joy to me, but my happiness was to be short-lived. The headaches and dizziness became more severe, and I collapsed with a cerebellum haemorrhage, a direct result of the accident.

I felt that God's hand was heavy upon me and I faced an empty and depressing future. My condition had deteriorated considerably, and I suffered further periods in hospital and nursing home. It was then that I was told that there was no hopeful future for me; the doctors shook their heads and talked about a Home for the Disabled. There was much time for thinking, and I could foresee no purpose or guidance in my life. All I could do was to leave myself in God's Hands—maybe He would show me a purpose. I was handed a poem and I realised that it contained a hard and difficult lesson that I had to learn:—

> I laid down in silence this work of mine;
> For God had sent to me a resting time.
> I took rest and stillness from His own Hand,
> Trusting the illness was as He planned.
>
> There's a blessed peace in lying still,
> Letting God's Hand mould, as He will;
> His work to complete, His lessons set;
> He calls for obedience, lest I forget.
>
> I'm in His Hands, I must be trained,
> I have to learn by sufferings gained.
> His yoke is easy, His burden light,
> His discipline needful—and all is right.
>
> I am just His servant, I cannot choose
> If this tool or that His Hand shall use.
> In working, or resting, may I fulfil
> Not mine at all but my Master's will.
>
> Clare Wadley.

I pondered this message earnestly and prayed for a new purpose. My prayers did not, however, appear to receive an answer and I became more and more depressed. I shrank from the thought of entering a

Home for the Disabled, feeling that it would precipitate the end of my life.

My family were very concerned about my plight, and my brother was particularly troubled. After very serious consideration and consultation with his wife, he decided to offer me a haven within his own home. It was not a very big house and there was a growing family in it, but there was a semi-basement room that I could have, and I gladly accepted it. When I arrived I discovered the loving kindness which had been lavished upon me. Some of my own furniture had been assembled so that I might feel more at home. It was a room where I could make a separate home yet be near my family. I was not able to cook for myself, so my sister-in-law took on this task and brought food down to me on a tray when I was not well enough to eat with the family. I was grateful but very unhappy.

One Good Friday morning I was alone in the house, the family having gone to church. My resources of faith and courage were very, very low indeed and I was sorely distressed when, in the silence, I heard a voice quietly but distinctly addressing me. It was hardly audible at first, but as I adjusted my thoughts its message came to me loud and clear. "You will recover," it said. "But how? but how?" I anxiously asked. Great joy was now flooding into my soul as I heard the reply, "You must go to a Home of Healing. It is there you will find spiritual refreshment and strength."

When the family returned from church my brother found me in a state of great excitement. I told him what had happened. I was convinced that the Good Shepherd had Himself spoken to me. My brother listened with every sympathy and we prayed together. I did not know if such a Home existed, and if it did would they accept me, a hopeless invalid?

Then followed many sleepless nights for my brother and myself. We could not find the right solution; but the Almighty intervened again. I came across a letter from Miss Nora Hawkes. I had met her in a nursing home after my accident. She had just undergone a major operation and was convalescing, and in her letter told me of the comfort and help she had received at a Healing Fellowship. I immediately wrote to her begging for further information.

By return of post I received a reply. She had been to the Crowhurst Home of Healing in Sussex, and after I had stated my case to the Principal it was not long before I was on my way. My strength was at its very lowest ebb. I was an ambulance case. But what a happy day it was when I left my little room, though I was very thankful and appreciative of the love and help I had received.

I was already quite sure that a Home of Divine Healing was much to be preferred to a Home for Incurables. I prayed, thanking the Lord with a very grateful heart.

CHAPTER 2

Crowhurst and Resthaven

*They met constantly to hear the apostles teach, and to share the
common life, to break bread, and to pray.
A sense of awe was everywhere . . .*

Acts 2.42 N.E.B.

I REMEMBER VERY LITTLE of my journey. I know I
was in pain most of the time. I could see the
reflections of London and sounds of traffic; then
gradually I felt the sweet peace of the countryside as
we sped into Sussex.

Crowhurst is near Battle. The Home is surrounded
by gardens and woods. I did not see them then as it
was dark when I arrived. When the ambulance door
was opened I was greeted by a smiling lady worker.
The front door was open and a friendly light was
shining through.

My physical condition caused some consternation. I
had found it difficult to scrape together the smallest
fees, so my room was a tiny one. The ambulance
attendants got me to it and I collapsed exhausted on
the bed. I stayed there for two days, and it was not
until the third day that I was conscious of the
presence of Howard Cobb, the Founder and first
Warden of the Home. He appeared at my door in a
blue robe. I was afterwards to learn that this was the
colour of healing. He was tall, lean and grey-haired,
with gentle, penetrating eyes. There was great serenity about him, of which I was aware from the moment

14

he opened the door. He talked quietly for a few minutes, then put his hand on my head and blessed me. I felt very comforted.

Howard Cobb's life itself had been very unusual. He was an Anglican vicar who had been brought into the Ministry of Healing in a remarkable way. While serving as a parish priest he had become seriously ill, and his doctors said he could not survive. His wife had borne him up in prayer, and called in James Moore Hickson for healing—and Howard Cobb made a wonderful recovery. He was convinced of his healing and felt compelled to pursue a Healing Ministry. His Bishop gave him permission to start a Home, and Crowhurst—the first of the Healing Homes in England, was the result.

There was a strong atmosphere of peace and fellowship there. I soon discovered that many sick, crippled and sorrowful had received so many blessings. The whole spiritual environment was new and very challenging to me. When I was able to get about I had the first of several private talks with Howard Cobb. He asked me why I had come to Crowhurst, and what I hoped to gain from my visit. I said that I hoped to be healed. His challenging question set me thinking. Would I gain anything from this visit even if I were not made whole again?

God had indeed guided me to this wonderful Home where there was such great spiritual power through human fellowship. I knew then that I must endeavour to *give* as well as *receive*.

My condition was causing me much embarrassment. I lacked co-ordination; I was falling down a great deal; and finding the stairs very difficult though

I struggled to negotiate them. The simple process of guiding my food to my mouth was sometimes impossible, when much of it could finish up on my lap! I could not remember things, and there was considerable alarm among the other guests one afternoon when I fell into a low table set for afternoon tea, and sent everything flying. This brought things to a climax, for I was feeling utterly defeated. I was helped to my room and prayed with great urgency for help.

My money was running out and I should have to leave very soon. I was not much better. Howard Cobb heard of my fall and he came to see me. He arranged that I should be one of those to be ministered to in the forthcoming Service of Healing in the small but beautiful Chapel. Its furnishings were simple; just a small altar and cross, kneeling rail, chairs and organ. It was the focal point of the Home, a truly holy place. Howard Cobb's life was enveloped with prayer, and he spent a large part of his time in the Chapel. It was here that he was strengthened with power to face the daily difficulties that confronted him.

I can remember that service so well. One by one we made our painful way to the altar and knelt in humble supplication before the Almighty. The prayerful, powerful hands of Howard Cobb were placed on each one in turn. They pressed heavily upon me and I felt a great surge of power. There was a tingling sensation in my head and down my spine. A cold and cleansing force filled me, and this was driven out by an even greater burning, thrusting fire. I felt a deep sense of joy and release and great relief. Howard Cobb lifted his hands from my head. I was convinced that I was completely healed. I rose from my knees feeling radiant and fulfilled. When the service was over I returned to my room unaided; and when the door was closed I actually skipped!

But I soon realised that I was not completely cured, although I was immeasurably better. Many days of instruction and quiet preparation followed, spent in waiting upon the Lord in expectation of another Service of Healing when I hoped I would again experience the outflow of His Sacramental Grace.

I realised that I was enveloped within the spiritual fellowship of the Home, and slowly gained an increasing knowledge of the depth and power to be found there, and that this was an extension of the Churches' Ministry to the World. I discovered that in addition to physical healing the Spirit of Christ was available to bring release from the problems and sins of mankind —and that this release could contribute to the physical healing. As I continued to attend the services my condition improved, but it became clear to me that I had taken only the first step in a long, difficult, upward climb. My money was now running very short, and I would have to leave and return to my basement room. How I longed to stay! Howard Cobb noticed my sadness and realised the reason for it. When we talked about it I told him I was aware that I still needed so much from the Ministry of Healing. He listened very sympathetically, and to my intense gladness asked me if I would stay on for a longer period, helping with light secretarial duties, paying a smaller fee and sharing in the Healing Grace of the Home.

As my physical condition improved I became more

17

responsible and when the Secretary went on holiday I deputised for her. This gave me a further and very valuable insight into the Ministry. Howard Cobb's life was dedicated to prayer, and staff and patients were closely involved with it. He exerted a discipline on the corporate group that moulded, inspired and influenced us, and during my privileged life at Crowhurst I saw many who received this blessing. When healed in body and spirit they went out and were guided to the work to which God was calling them. I prayed that I also might receive my call.

I must quote one incident. Edna Graver went to Crowhurst to prepare to die; she had a severe spinal condition which was said to be terminal. Mr. Cobb helped her by prayer and instruction, but neither was thinking in terms of physical healing. One day she said to him, "My spine feels much stronger, I would like to get up." Medical advice was sought, she was given permission, and found that she was able to walk about the house and gardens. The next day she walked to the village, and continued to make excellent progress every day. When she left she started a Home for mongol children near Minehead, and the story of that Home is another amazing proof of the Guidance and Love of the Healing Christ.

The time came at last when I had to leave. I was most grateful for the many blessings received, the rich fellowships made, and the lessons learned, but I had not received a call to service. So I returned to my basement room. I was at a dead end, and there seemed no promising future, for while I was conscious of much physical improvement I was still a long way from being able to earn my living.

It was then that God again intervened in a wonderful and unexpected way. I received an invitation to spend two weeks at another Home of Healing as a guest. The strange thing is that I cannot remember the name of the person who extended the invitation, and I would not recognise her face if I met her in the street! The astonishing results which were to develop out of this kindness were to bring me again into the stream of the Ministry of Healing. Most important of all, it was one of the strands which helped me later to find my own destiny.

The name of this Home was Resthaven. It is in beautiful Cotswold country. When I arrived it seemed like one of the Courts of Heaven, for it was so peaceful. The staff were so very kind and helpful. The Founder and first Warden was Miss Maud Carruthers Little, and when my fortnight was over she asked me if I would like to stay on a little longer, as "part patient and part staff". She may have heard of my work in a similar capacity at Crowhurst. I was overjoyed. I must confess that at the beginning I was "patient" for about twenty-two hours a day and "staff" for the remaining two. Gradually I was able to devote more time to secretarial duties.

Miss Little had herself been a patient at a sanatorium. She recovered, but felt that in her treatment not enough emphasis had been laid on "wholeness and health". She was a vegetarian, and on her discharge returned to her home in Pitchcombe, near Stroud. She daily climbed a hill near Pitchcombe, and there she prayed that she might be allowed to found a Vegetarian Home for Health and Healing. She prayed for more than twenty years

19

before the miracle happened. She had collected all the financial help that her friends and relatives could provide, and with this money she was able to buy part of the hill upon which she had prayed so long, and build the Home she called Resthaven.

During her time of waiting and preparation she had met James Moore Hickson, a Church of England layman who had been given the power of healing, and was instrumental in the recovery of Howard Cobb. James Moore Hickson stayed in the family home, and Miss Little had been privileged to watch him administer his special gifts of God in her own village. Thus there was a link for me between those Homes, for they had both been inspired by this truly remarkable and godly man.

We were a very happy band at Resthaven. Maud Little led us with calm and confident direction. How hard working she was! Many days she was the first in the kitchen, baking a large batch of wholemeal bread. She also had oversight of the gardens where most of the fruit and vegetables used in the Home were grown. When her supervisory work was done she would return to her office to deal with the considerable correspondence and administrative duties. The most important part of her day was given over to the care of the sick and needy in the Home. Resthaven was at that time a registered nursing home and some of the patients required—and received—very skilled nursing. The "centre" of the Home was the Chapel where daily services were taken and private prayer was encouraged.

Brother Mandus gave a Healing service at Resthaven. One of those sharing the Ministry was

Marjorie. She was badly crippled with arthritis, spending most of her day in her chair, or hobbling awkwardly with two sticks. At the service Brother Mandus met her at the door, helped her out of the chair, took her arm and gently walked her up and down. It was obvious that she was in great pain. Slowly she began to straighten up, dropped her stick, and to our amazement, walked out of the Chapel at the end, quite unaided. For several days she was without her sticks, but a bad migraine attack forced her to bed, and it took her some time to regain her confidence. It was, however, really inspiring later to see her go down to the vegetable garden, put in some work there, and then take up other duties in the house, and we rejoiced with her in her new lease of life.

Shortly after my arrival, Mrs. Mary Thomas came as a patient. Soon we began to try to help other patients, and with Pauline, and Sister Jane, we formed a "foursome". Maud Little was so pleased with what we were doing that she decided to take a much-needed holiday and leave us in charge. We were naturally thrilled and felt a very high sense of vocation and much humility.

I spent five very happy years at Resthaven. It certainly was a veritable haven of rest and healing for me, but it was three years before I was strong enough to venture out on my own. I knew, of course, that I would never be fully cured, but God had taught me how to live with myself and to bear my pain and suffering. The great day came, however, when I was able to get on a bus and take a train journey without assistance.

It is impossible to say how much I owe to Howard Cobb and Maud Little, and how privileged I was to be brought into fellowship with them. I envied the utter dependence they had on their Lord. From the early days when Maud Little had climbed the hill at Pitchcombe she had acquired the capacity to relate her obedience and trust to the Good Shepherd, and this capacity was also very much in evidence in the life of Howard Cobb.

The Holy Spirit was now working more in my life, and making me more conscious of the guidance of the Loving Shepherd. He was teaching me to give Him more of my time and obedience by listening to His Voice. I was beginning to question my motives, and to keep a more steadfast eye upon Him, realising that my willingness to serve Him must be the key of my quest. Yes! His Hand was heavy upon me, but in a new and joyful way I was in awesome anticipation of his Plan and Purpose for me. The time spent in these Homes had been a period of quiet preparation for the next stage, and now I felt I was ready for it.

CHAPTER 3

Knowing by Doing

Lord God Almighty, guide us to Thy Will;
Steadfast our minds to do Thy will; That we may inwardly love
Thee before all things—with a pure mind.
For Thou art our Maker and Redeemer.
Praise and glory be to Thee now, Ever and ever without end.
King Alfred A.D. 849-901.

DURING MY LAST YEAR at Resthaven my increased mobility had allowed me to extend my knowledge of the work of the Healing Ministry. I was inquiring everywhere, and attended meetings and conferences. For me the most important was at High Leigh, Hertfordshire, under the auspices of the London Healing Ministry. Under Maud Little's guidance I was spending part of each day in prayer and quiet supplication. There was no one present with me in the little Chapel there when something completely unexpected took place, and I look back upon it with awe and deep humility. I heard the Voice of the Good Shepherd again! The Voice commanded me to start another Home of Divine Healing. I was to find help among my friends in the Free Church. This was the guidance of God, and my future was being prepared.

During the rest of my stay and later in Free Church circles, I mentioned the matter to several leading Free Church Ministers and laymen. I received quite a shock when I heard them rebuff me:

"Ridiculous."

"What a foolish notion."

"Quite impossible."

"Forget it."

These and other discouraging remarks were from those who were supposed to be in sympathy with the work of Healing. What chance had I of convincing others? I contemplated my predicament and had to sympathise with my critics. The situation did in fact seem quite ridiculous and impossible, for this desire was being expressed by someone who was just managing to get about after years of incapacity, with no money and of little importance!

When I returned to Resthaven I discussed the matter with Maud Little. She was certain that God had spoken to me. Her advice was to rely utterly upon Him, to probe and pray, and to face the challenge realistically. She, of all people, had found from experience that "Whoever will do the Will of God shall know the teaching . . .". I read and re-read John, chapter 7, verse 17, and from this knowledge led the action.

I remember that there had been one person at High Leigh who had sympathised with me, Dr. A. D. Belden, D.D., a Congregational Minister. I wrote to him, and in his reply he told me that this was a project that he had longed to see reach fruition. We agreed that it was of God and that we should pray very earnestly for guidance and wisdom. Within a few months we had a small committee to pray with us, help promote our fund-raising and look for premises. We were also blessed with some support from the medical profession, for many doctors were beginning to acknowledge that the stresses of life were bound up with a number of illnesses, and that faith and prayer could be a most potent panacea. Mr. Griffith Evans, M.A., D.M., an eminent Fellow of the Royal College of Surgeons, agreed to become Joint Chairman with Dr. Belden; our committee was really beginning to move. The various denominations were represented by the Rev. J. Jones, Rev. and Mrs. Maurice Buckley, Sister Elsie Chapple, Eric Bales and others.

Progress was, however, very slow. It was the mid-1950's and the general attitude to healing and health was quite different from what it is now. I became quite impatient. I wanted to get on. The funds for the work were coming in very slowly. Nevertheless, we pressed on in faith. An estate agent had been consulted, and Dr. Belden and I were travelling to see different properties. There seemed to be very few which fitted our needs. They were either too big and derelict or too small. When the agent mentioned a property near Bournemouth I nearly decided not to see it; I had the vision of houses very much sought after and very expensive. Our guidance, however, was to go and we found just the house we were looking for in a lovely wooded spot called Branksome Park. This area had been developed in the late 19th-century with large houses, each individually planned and standing in its own extensive grounds. By the 1930's they were fast becoming too large for domestic use, and there were some on the market at "knock-down" figures.

The house was spacious but ugly, with heavy red brick Victorian architraves. It had a lovely peaceful garden, and I was specially charmed with the wood-panelled library, which could be made so easily into a small Chapel. We immediately offered rather less than the asking price, and this was accepted. I could now find the money for the deposit, for after years of negotiation I received £500 compensation from the car manufacturers responsible for my accident. I had also an interest-free loan of £1000, and we were allowed to take out a mortgage at reasonable interest.

We returned to London and told the Executive what we had done! After some apprehension—we had no money for furniture or upkeep—it was agreed that we should go forward, trusting the Good Shepherd to show us the next step.

It was a case of "stepping out with God." I knew we were within His Guiding Hand. Within a few days we were told that a friend would underwrite our account at the bank to the extent of £300. It is entirely to God's glory that we never drew on this money. From somewhere or other our wants were alway provided, and the loan was made into a definite gift.

Back at Resthaven I told Miss Little about the turn of events. As ever she was full of helpful suggestions; she arranged a collection in the Chapel, and with this money we were able to buy some of the bare necessities for opening the new Home. She also said she would see me settled in, and generously offered the help of Inga Lill and Mariette, two Swedish girls who were helping at Resthaven. They had a few months longer before they were due to return home, and they were young and prepared to help with the heavy work. On March 28, 1955 we all set off to take up residence.

On arrival Maud Little produced a large casserole of home grown vegetables and herbs, with crusty bread baked in her own oven. We ate it at a small, rough garden table, with a towel for a tablecloth and one knife between us! We had a minimum of furniture, the house was bitterly cold as there was no heating. There were some very poorly equipped beds, but we managed to survive the night in coats and scarves; and the first thing next morning we bought blankets and other vital goods.

On our return our first guest had arrived—Kit Hodges. She had spent many years in a wheel-chair, and I had become very friendly with her at Resthaven. She had told me she wished to be our first guest, and I gladly accepted the idea; the money she could afford would help us buy some of the necessities required. I had not expected that her enthusiasm would draw her to us so soon. I found her a most cheering companion. It was amazing what she could do to help.

That day a solicitor called to say that there was some legal complication relating to the purchase of the property; apparently it did not yet belong to us, and we would have to pay twenty pounds a week rent until matters were cleared. This was a serious blow, but somehow we paid it for the next eight weeks. How we managed to get the money has always remained a mystery!

Even though the sense of God's guidance was so strong there were times when we nearly lost faith. It was such a frustrating time; I had a van load of furniture in London, and this could not be delivered until the legal formalities had been overcome. I had in store an electric iron, sewing machine and many other things we badly needed which we could have used to great advantage, but we spent the time instead in cleaning and re-decorating. It was a day of much rejoicing when we were told that the property was at last legally ours.

That night when the others had gone to bed I went into every room asking for God's richest blessing on the new undertaking which we hoped to dedicate to His Glory and the blessing of the sick. Our first Chaplain, the Rev. Ian Hope, took a special Dedication Service of the little panelled room that was to be the Chapel, and from that day we held daily services. I placed a new book on the altar we had constructed, and in this book would be written the names of those who were sent to us. It remained there the whole of the time I was in residence. Every month, every week, and sometimes every day, a new name or names were added.

I was indeed truly thankful and grateful to God, for I was richly blessed, and I realised that He was the Good Shepherd and had given us many glimpses of his Love and the abundance of His Grace. We had given a lot of thought and prayer to the naming of the Home, and when one of our first guests who had received great blessing and healing, suggested "Green Pastures" we turned to the twenty-third Psalm, feeling how appropriate it was.

During our very early days I had asked Inga Lill and Mariette, the Swedish girls, if they had ever been to a Jumble Sale. They had not. We went to one in a local church hall, and they quickly understood its purpose, for we were short of almost everything. There was a wide variety of things for sale, mostly for a few pence. The girls got very excited, and were soon launched on what to us was a spending spree. Inga

Lill said to me, "Sister Ruth, there is a large tea-pot here, we do need it," while Mariette rushed up to exclaim, "Look at this useful tray I've just bought." We walked home loaded like tinkers, with useful objects which were quickly put to use. This was the first of several sales, and my success led me to be adventurous enough to attend a carpet and furniture auction. I watched the bidding, and rather shyly put in a bid for a kitchen gadget we badly needed. It was knocked down to me, and later a vacuum cleaner was mine for a reasonable figure. I now had the taste of success and a very good bedroom chair was soon acquired.

It was a two-days sale and I had arrived late on the first day but next morning I was there quite early with my luncheon sandwiches, prepared to "camp out" in the sale room if necessary, for there were many things listed which I hoped to bid for. The auctioneer's man eyed me with suspicion when the bidding stopped for the luncheon period—and he decided to lock me in! There were some quite valuable items in the room and I was obviously suspected! At the end I had a complete vanload of most useful possessions. I bought some second-hand pieces of stair carpet for twelve shillings. Some of it was threadbare, but we darned the pattern in with coloured wools, and it was laid on the stairs; it lasted for two years, and there were sections of it in the house years later.

The time arrived for Inga Lill and Mariette to return to Sweden. Their help had been invaluable, and as I saw them off at the railway station they were both weeping, for they wished they could have stayed longer. They had both been wonderful to me and both admitted that their stay had been one of the happiest times of their lives. Kit Hodges was also leaving as she had other claims. She had been a fine friend, and it was amazing to dwell upon the many-sided activities she had been able to do from her wheel chair. I was very sad as these dear friends left. I realised how much I needed a dedicated staff, so asked the Good Shepherd to send the right people that the Home should develop according to His Plan and Purpose.

We could not afford to pay much in salaries, but again God provided, and He sent those who could help us on to the next step.

Guests had been coming from our earliest days —well before we were really able to deal with them, but within a short time we were full to capacity. The work was hard and carried out under high pressure. I was very much better, working hard and in reasonable health, but I did find walking a problem. I really needed a small car. We prayed about it, and made the need known, but there was no response. Some time later I received a letter from an invalid who had spent all her adult life in one room. Recently a friend had brought her some flowers wrapped in an old newspaper in which she had read of our need for a car. When she heard that our need had not been met, she supplied sufficient money for one! I was very grateful for this gift and the generosity and unselfishness behind it.

The first year passed very quickly. In May 1956 when I prepared the first Annual Report I was happily able to state that one hundred and forty guests and patients had stayed in the Home, and that many letters of thanks had been received for the blessings obtained. I was also able to report that the furniture and equipment had been considerably improved, and that we were out of debt. We had £200 in the bank! How this came about was, and still is, a mystery to me. We gathered in our little Chapel to give thanks to God for His supply.

CHAPTER 4

Abundant Grace

And in union with Christ Jesus He raised us up . . . so that He might display . . . how immense are the resources of His Grace, and how great is His kindness to us.

Ephesians 2.6-7 N.E.B.

ONE OF THE MOST AMAZING things about the first year of the Home was how the finance became available. We felt strongly that the Home was under the guidance of the Living Shepherd, but our vision was known only to a handful of praying people. The gifts that came in were sometimes from completely unexpected quarters.

As mentioned earlier, a friend had made us the loan of a thousand pounds, and we had thanked God for it. Later she wrote, with considerable embarrassment, that she had sent this money on such a sacrificial level that she had not left herself enough to buy food, and asked us to *lend* her a few pounds. We wanted to send more than she requested, but she would not accept it. When her acute need was over she returned the money, saying that the thousand pounds was now a gift and not a loan!

I found, however, that I had a severe financial problem to settle. I had "loaned" the £500 received as compensation for my accident, and while I had been willing to give God my strength, and He had multiplied it to meet the many demands made upon it, I found it very difficult to "give" this money, for it indicated in my mind security in old age. After a mental struggle lasting several weeks the Grace of the Good Shepherd enabled me to make it an outright gift. I was doubly recompensed in later years.

Our fees were kept at a very modest level. We believed that it was God's Home, and if anyone could not pay fully, we would accept half or even less than half of the fees. Despite this—or was it because of this rule?—we were always able to pay the bills, and in giving our ALL to Him we learned the miracle of supply. We knew Him to be the Good Shepherd, and that His Eye of Love was upon us.

It soon became evident that the house was not big enough. The dining room was overcrowded, and the one room I had kept for myself was office and general odd job room for sewing, painting furniture and other renovations; my bed was the least important article in the room.

We had another great disadvantage; there was only one ground floor bedroom, and many of our guests could not easily manage stairs. This fact became obvious enough when three severely handicapped people applied for accommodation at the same time. They all needed ground floor rooms. We were faced with a dilemma. Should we give the room to a woman straight from hospital who was suffering from a severe heart condition, or offer it to a man badly crippled with arthritis, or to a young man who could manage stairs only on his hands and knees?

We had just got out of debt. It seemed such hard work to start all over again, but we did need the accommodation. The staff prayed in the little Chapel, asking for His Guiding Hand to shew us the way. I was soon to discover the wonders of his abundant Grace. I was awakened very early one morning with the command, "Go forward in trust." In an instant I was given a vision of what I should do. There must be several more ground floor bedrooms, with provision for more on the first floor, and an enlarged Chapel and dining room—some of it to be completed at a later date. I also realised that I should consult a friendly building contractor, and when we discussed the matter later that day he listened very sympathetically. He had a son who was training to be an architect and who quickly drew up the plans.

The problem before me and the Executive was to decide how much of the scheme we could afford to proceed with. In view of the miraculous guidance of the first few years it was decided to go forward in faith with the immediate construction of the ground floor rooms.

Again we were soon made aware of the guidance of the Loving Shepherd. When a start was made we began to receive practical and financial assistance. We opened a Building Fund account, and our financial resources steadily grew.

The great day arrived when the builders were to begin. Their first task was to erect a large tent just outside the front door. They explained that quite a large portion of the existing rear premises would be uninhabitable during the building period, and the tent was to act as a store house. They then knocked down the larder and vegetable and dry goods stores, and the next few months the coal and the corn flakes rested side by side, divided by a thin sheet of canvas!

The foundations for the new annexe were quickly

dug, and concrete laid to support the brick walls. The foreman was a true craftsman and very proud of his work. When the first load of bricks arrived, he announced that I was to be given the privilege of laying the first one. The mortar was mixed and after a few practice runs I plumbed the first brick into position. As a matter of fact I finally laid about a dozen before the bricklayer decided that perhaps he should take over in the cause of expedience! Those bricks were eventually covered, but I have longed to dig away the earth that covers them to look at them again.

As the building grew we were discussing a date for the opening Dedication. The building contractor said that the work would be completed by the end of March, but I allowed an extra month, and we agreed in the Executive that April 30, 1960, should be the great day. A number of officials and civic dignitaries pencilled the date in their diaries. We had not allowed, however, for the uncertainties of the building industry, and soon the work seemed to slow down to a snail's pace. We were keeping the Home running but it became more and more difficult as the workmen took over more of the house, and my room began to look more like a junk shop than ever. This room was to become the new dining room, but it could not be converted until I had vacated it. There was no spare bed anywhere, and the only free space was in the Chapel. My bed was, therefore, moved into it. Office and other equipment, and the new furniture arriving daily, were also stacked there. At the end I could allocate myself only a square of about eighteen inches in which to dress and undress, and even this was gained by piling things on the bed. All the services were carried through faithfully, though we had to transfer them for the time into the lounge.

When the day of Dedication arrived it was beautiful and sunny. We were up at dawn as there was much to be done. There were carpets to lay, furniture to move, and much preparation to be done in the kitchen. There was a smell of new paint very prevalent, some of the paint dangerously wet.

Just before the ceremony I went with a friend to my new bathroom in the wing to tidy up. We were so engrossed with the business of the day that we forgot that there were no handles on the door. We closed it, soon to find that we could not open it. We shouted for help, various ladies came into the corridor and tried to release us with nail files and hairpins, but to no avail. There was only one solution—we should have to leave by the window; but the window was very small and neither of us could be called slim! I asked for two stools, one was manoeuvred through the window to us and the other left outside. I then pushed my friend through to the best of my ability, while the ladies pulled. We eventually got her through, and I followed with difficulty. Many times after, I looked at that window and wondered how we had accomplished such a feat. A large crowd had gathered to see the fun!

We joined in thanking God for our wonderful Dedication; there were greetings from near and far, and great rejoicing when it was announced that most of the money for the wing had already been raised. Mr. Griffith Evans, who spoke at this Thanksgiving Service, said, "The Healing Ministry is for the restoration of the whole being. It shows God's Love in action, and is the most powerful channel of evangelism."

The building of the first new annexe had been another treasured and wonderful experience for me. I was again carried forward on wings of joy and faith.

We were now able to provide a small Counselling room, and later a two-room sun lounge, which was a godsend to those unable to get about much. We had also rented a beach chalet at Branksome Chine. It was a happy day when our first guests were taken for a rest and a meal by the sea. The Home remained full, with very little advertising. Churches sent their convalescent members, guests sent their friends, and some came time and time again.

The Executive now gave me another small car, partly in lieu of the salary I often had not taken. Our Sub-Warden used the first and it made shopping and getting our guests down to the sea much easier. So we were being led forward, one step at a time. The gifts we had offered to God had been blessed, and He had used and multiplied them so many times. We had asked for His Guidance, and then gone forward into the unknown in love and obedience, and He was constantly adding substance to the vision we had received from Him.

CHAPTER 5

Staff

> *May the warmth and light of Thine own Healing*
> *Power radiate through all Thy Homes of Healing*
> *that they may be as beacons of light, drawing to Thee*
> *all who need Thy touch.*
>
> Resthaven prayer.

WHEN INGA LILL, Mariette and Kit Hodges
departed they left behind them very happy
memories. I have already mentioned that we were
blessed by the staff that followed them. Some saw
something of the vision we had, and they helped
practically to bring it into being. There have been so
many devoted workers that I can mention only a few
of them. I must, however, pay tribute to all, giving
thanks for the contributions and the sacrifices they
made, for very small salaries; some even gave voluntary service. Staff accommodation was poor at first,
but I do not remember much grumbling about this.
We were able later to give better rooms and more
privacy.

There were many problems. Sometimes guests
were difficult; there were also very sick people to cope

with, and awkward jobs to do, but the staff radiated love and kindness most of the time. There were, of course, days when things went wrong and tempers were frayed, but reconciliation soon took place with prayer and goodwill. One such occasion I remember very well. I was just about to take a Service of Healing which meant a time of special preparation and prayer. Before the service one of the staff had an unexpected and very bad outburst of temper. It upset me so badly that I was shaking, and felt it was impossible to carry on. People were waiting in the Chapel so I just had to continue. The only thing to do was to hand the position over to the Good Shepherd. Still trembling I began in prayer. In a few moments it seemed as if my little "self" had been completely pushed aside so that the Holy Spirit could work through me unhindered. Many afterwards referred to the sense of awe and special blessing that enveloped them. I also learnt a special lesson through this incident, and feeling that I may have contributed to the outburst of temper I made it my business to find my colleague. By this time she was feeling in the wrong, and we gladly forgave each other.

When Inga Lill and Mariette returned to Sweden they told their friends about the Home, and we had many offers of help from that and other countries. The large majority of the foreign girls were charming and competent. They arrived usually for the holiday season which made vacations for our permanent staff an easier proposition.

Not all our foreign workers were young. I well remember a charming married couple from Switzerland. The husband had a good medical degree and his wife was also a graduate. They were allowed to do only domestic work in England, but came here to improve their English and agreed to stay for several months. I often wished to talk to them about themselves, but they were very withdrawn, and I detected a great sadness in them. They had spent only half of their time with us when they came into my office. The man was full of smiles and the woman looked radiant. They asked if they could leave at once. They wished to travel home immediately. They had been advised that they could never have children, and their visit to Green Pastures was a result of receiving this sad news. They had decided to make a fresh start without children of their own, and their desire to learn English was bound up with the hope of serving and helping children in other lands. I realised why they had seemed so sad, but their short stay with us had produced a miracle and the wife became pregnant! She was advancing in years and their desire was to get home for expert attention and to await the treasured arrival. We were delighted to let them go, though sorry to lose them, and so thankful that the Green Pastures' blessing had fallen on them. Later, they let us know of the birth of a fine healthy boy.

Another incident was linked with a Dutch girl. She was engaged to a Dutchman, but they both wanted an English wedding. She showed me the white wedding dress in her wardrobe. All the money she had brought to England equalled about two pounds; and she wanted the ceremony in church with music and flowers. There was also the hint of a reception! The day arived, the bridegroom arrived, rather shy and overawed. A bouquet was made, the bride looked

radiant, and I was Matron of Honour at the ceremony. Cook had made a lovely cake, and after the
reception the couple went off together on his motor
cycle. The bride had never ridden pillion before, and
their first few moments of married life were certainly
a test of partnership! The following year they
brought a fine baby to show us.

"Grimmy" was a guest in the early days and stayed
on to give voluntary service; and then accepted our
"pocket-money salary" for several years. I recall the
hilarious laughter each Christmas which came from
the crippled children to whom we gave a party, which
she organised; and there was always a wonderful
surprise for them. I shall never forget the rapture on
those young faces. "Grimmy" was also very good with
our older guests, and often devoted some of her free
time reading to those unable to see.

Kathleen had faithfully nursed her mother for
twenty-six years and her father for seven. She collapsed, and was taken to hospital; and her mother
died about that time. Later, her church sent her to us,
and I was told that she could easily die, for there were
three serious physical troubles caused by severe
overstrain. The gentle loving Shepherd laid His
Hands upon her, and she recovered to give us several
years of loving faithful service, saying that those years
had been the happiest of her life. Later, she died in
my arms, as the hospital had sent her back as
incurable. The fuller Healing was to come to her the
other side of the veil.

Eva volunteered to do the cooking as our cook had
been taken ill. I asked her if she had much experience, and she said 'No! but I am going to pray as I

cook." She produced a most delicious Yorkshire pudding, and everyone asked for more. When I asked her what she had put in it, to my amazement she replied, "Just flour and water". So we came to the conclusion that her prayers had been answered, and that a hidden hand had added some "miracle" ingredient!

Jim was an old age pensioner who was so happy doing odd jobs in the kitchen and garden. His hands were badly crippled and he was slow in carrying out any task, but he just radiated joy and service. At one stage he discovered that the Home was short of money, and he handed over a considerable portion of his small savings. I kept this gift for a short time, then handed it back to him with our love and appreciation.

In the early days a nurse in a clearly exhausted state came to us. She had been doing very heavy night and morning nursing at a small nursing home. Her condition deteriorated and she became unconscious and had severe haemorrhage. Her doctor was very concerned, said the prognosis was bad, and that he would have her transferred to hospital the following morning. Some of us went to her room and prayed quietly and earnestly. Suddenly she regained consciousness. She was obviously much better and was asking for food. The doctor returned next morning, saying that the tests had proved his prognosis. I suggested she was much better and that he should see her. He examined her, and found that all the symptoms had disappeared. He looked at me quietly, then said, "This can only be the result of prayer. Keep her in bed for a day or two—and continue to pray."

She made a full recovery, joined our staff, served us devotedly and was much loved.

The staff usually attended the short morning service, often during the singing of the first hymn. Cook was nearly always the last to arrive, and she would stand at the back near the gas fire. I was not leading the service one morning, and I too was sitting at the back. I heard a gasp and looked up to see her apron ablaze. She was so stunned that she just stood and looked at the flames. Fortunately I was wearing a coat, which I took off and with which I smothered the flames and extinguished them but the experience was horrifying. It all happened so quickly that few of the worshippers were disturbed in their prayers. When I told people what had happened we held a special Service of Thanksgiving, and I saw to it that an extra safety guard was attached to the fire.

Elizabeth wrote, "In April, 1961, I was praying for guidance for the next step when I read about Green Pastures' need of helpers. I went there immediately, and said that while I had no experience of the Healing Ministry I was sure God was leading me into it, and was told to start the next day! What talks I had with Sister Ruth. I knew that if I needed help or advice there was an open invitation to go to her room." Since she left us, Elizabeth has been much used in the Healing Ministry. She had found our House a fruitful training ground.

Clare wrote, "For as long as I can remember, life had been hard and lonely; no family or loved ones; no home to which to return for holidays after strenuous work. Suffering from severe depression, feeling there was little in life for me in this existence, I went to Green Pastures as a patient. There I found deep peace and rest; a renewal of courage and spiritual power. But I could afford only a short stay, and was expecting to return to my dreaded lonely life when I was asked if I would become one of the helpers. How deeply and sincerely I thank the Loving Shepherd for those years of happy fellowship in service for others, and the beginning of a larger, fuller life than any I had previously experienced, and for which I can never adequately express my gratitude."

Vera, a most capable and helpful Sub-Warden, always endeavoured to get our guests to the chalet and the sea, however incapacitated they were, and she shared with me in some of the counselling work. One case she dealt with concerned a young married woman with two children; her marriage was breaking down. She had been in a mental hospital several times, and came for a time of rest and refreshment, to which she reacted very well. On her return home I promised to keep in touch with her. Several weeks later I was just starting my "off day", intending to visit some friends, when her image flashed across my mind, and I felt that I must go to her. I arrived somewhat apologetically at breakfast time. I could see immediately that something was wrong. "Thank God you have come, you are the answer to my prayer," she said. During the night she had made an abortive effort to end her life, and had resolved to carry through the plan as soon as the family had left home. Her husband now felt unable to cope with her and they were having bitter quarrels. I took her back to Green Pastures, leaving a note for the husband. He

44

followed that evening, when it was agreed that she should stay for several weeks. Provision was made for the children's welfare. Her condition slowly improved; she began to "blossom" within the new atmosphere. The husband visited her several times, and she began to realise how necessary she was to her husband and children. It was decided that there must be a fresh start to their marriage if there were to be any chance of success. On the final morning of her stay the husband arrived with the children; we prayed together for God's blessing, and as a final act they reconsecrated their marriage vows before the altar. They now have a happy life, and one daughter is serving in the Mission Field.

Janet, Florrie, Isobel, Ivy, Velma, Eva, Charles, Marjorie, Audrey, Owie and others—their names are written in letters of gold in the Book of Life. We learned to grow in strength together, finding that there was more abundant grace to draw upon as we endeavoured to serve the Loving Shepherd through His needy ones.

CHAPTER 6

The Guidance That Challenges

> *For our fight is not against human foes, but against cosmic powers, against the authorities and potentates of this dark world, against superhuman forces of evil.*
>
> Ephesians 6.12. N.E.B.

IT WAS NOT LONG after we had opened our doors to our first guests that a pattern emerged which did not change much during the years. The rules were "Breakfast in bed" and "No discussion in the lounge about personal ailments," but I was always available for private talks. The staff also had breakfast trays, but in fine weather they took them into the garden. There was much freedom of action for the guests, for they came for rest and recuperation, and there was the precious power of the Healing of the Great Shepherd always present. There was a daily service in the Chapel, but for many the climax was the weekly Healing service, often followed by Holy Communion.

I had to set aside a large part of each day for "listening and counselling". Previously I would pray that I could be a cleansed channel through which the Holy Spirit could work. Two easy chairs and a relaxed atmosphere helped to create peace and calm. I tried to keep very still that the Voice of the Shepherd could be heard; and I struggled to understand His purpose for the patients. For many the interview could be the climax of something started much earlier by the Holy Spirit. It was very awe-inspiring to know of the Power that sometimes came through. Sympathy and compassion were abundantly needed. Many guests had quite lost their bearings; others expected me to be available at any time—even in the night! With some, each session might be a repetition, and much patience was required in getting through this phase. It was a minor miracle in me, as I am by nature an impatient person! When the "unwinding" period was over we were able to take constructive steps.

We would pray together. I would pray first and then encourage a personal response from the sufferer. For many this was the first hesitant step in prayer since childhood, and it did not come easily. I then suggested private prayer in the Chapel; later still would follow the Healing service, with the Laying on of Hands. I also prayed that they would realise that they were in the very presence of the Great Shepherd Himself.

It was a fine and uplifting yet humbling experience to be aware that the Guiding Shepherd needed human hearts and hands to work through. The Home just had to be the place where peace and powerful prayer were the focal point, for patients had to be given the opportunity to look at life anew. They needed time to correct wrong attitudes, and to open up the shutters so that they could be delivered from the things that held them in bondage; then they would be free to receive the flow of Divine Love and Power which awaited their acceptance, and brought with it a renewal of life and a clearer vision.

It was often necessary to encourage the sufferers to think quietly about the burden of sin which stood to their debit before God and to ask for His forgiveness. It must be sadly recorded that lack of repentance often prevented a cure and caused a return of old troubles.

There was another lesson to be learned. There came a time when the lower self rebelled. There was an unconscious desire to prolong illness, and with it the privileges enjoyed, with a lesser responsibility towards life's demands. In these cases a definite effort of will was needed, for to seek only physical relief was to turn spiritual healing into something approaching magic. Body, mind and spirit are one complete whole, and the recovery and maintenance of health depended on a true balance being struck between them.

From the outset we decided that our diet should consist of wholesome food, and that an atmosphere of tranquillity should prevail. All were encouraged to take advantage of the natural beauty of the garden and the restful therapy of the sea, which, together with medical or nursing care, helped to create a balanced life.

It was absolutely essential that we should begin each day asking for the guidance of the Loving Shepherd. There were times when we were aware of His Presence, and life was full of joy; our daily activities were a continuous outburst of praise, and throughout the day we realised that we were being guided by Him.

It was not always easy, however, guidance often involving a willingness to be challenged and an acceptance of tribulation and difficulty. We had our misfortunes and problems, our shocks and sad times. Once I was asked to take a teenager whose mother had died while she was a baby. As a schoolgirl she had given birth to an illegitimate child. Would I give her a fresh beginning? What an opportunity to bring her to Christ! We loved and cherished her—and she rewarded us by stealing from the guests and staff!

There were times when our peaceful atmosphere was singled out for attack by some sort of evil. On one occasion a woman guest came for a fortnight. Soon the staff were reporting peculiar noises in the night, and even some of the guests realised that something was amiss. I was convinced that the woman had brought evil into the Home, and I spent much time in prayer asking for safety and protection. Our Chaplain, whom I consulted, was nonplussed; and finding my account difficult to accept he questioned other members of the staff whose opinion concurred with mine. During one night I went outside the door of every guest room and prayed for cleansing and protection. On the woman's departure the atmosphere improved and we gave thanks. I wrote to a friend who knew her and described the situation; she replied that the same thing had happened elsewhere. There was an evil influence in her life and we had kept it under control by constant prayer but had not been able to help further. I felt that we had failed badly, but as she refused to attend any of the services or enter into our prayer life, we could only leave her in God's hands.

Our power-house was the Chapel. Many realised that the Healing Shepherd was in our midst. I had started to take a service, feeling tired and with nothing to give, but found that He always was there to give what was needed. I often witnessed the answer to prayer, and saw many raised up by faith in Him to receive the vision and obey His will.

There were many who came to Green Pastures but did not receive a complete healing, though it was very seldom that they went away without a spiritual cleansing, and with peace and strength to face the future.

"I must tell you of the great spiritual experience I had," wrote one of the guests on returning home. "I found the whole atmosphere of the Chapel was alight with the love of God. It has been the greatest inspiration of my life; I left filled with love, peace and power."

The Healing service that took place in the Chapel followed very much the pattern which had brought me such relief at Crowhurst. The focal point there was the "Laying on of hands". At times it was my moving privilege to be the instrument or channel of the Great Shepherd. I spent some time in prayer before the service, and sincerely dedicated myself to bestow the blessing. What a great occasion it was when both the sufferer and I felt the power of His Healing Love! Sometimes there was a warm glow, penetrating to every part of the body, while at other times there was a sharp urgent thrusting, or heavy vibration.

We developed a sense of the constant presence of the Lord, and I acquired a special awareness when there was serious need. On several occasions, especially in the middle of the night, I would be drawn to someone in great distress. I would don my dressing gown and slippers, and walk the silent corridors, and when the emergency was over would return to my room with a deep feeling of awe.

We had a few deaths. To some the great release gave much serenity and a knowledge that they were in the Hands of God. Those were the happy ones; but there were more who feared death. I was constantly surprised at the number of Christians in that category. There was a missionary who came to us under great stress and tension, knowing that her body was wearing out. She was consumed with dread; and we gave her much prayerful thought. When her time came to leave this world she was ready and had become completely transformed.

How important it is to think clearly about these matters! Our earthly bodies are given to us only for a short time. They are the outward garments of an eternal life. I was to see many "tattered garments" during those years. Some had inherited a very poor physique from their forebears; others had mental weaknesses that were hard to control. Wrong methods of thinking and living had also had their effect in some cases—and to many the visit of the Angel of Death was the greatest healing of all.

It is difficult to understand why all are not cured by His Healing Grace. At times the very saints of God do not seem to get an answer to their prayers. The Healing Ministry teaches that God deals differently with each individual, and that there is often a purpose He desires to accomplish through suffering. Jesus did not suffer from illness, but in God's Providence He did suffer the agony of the Cross, and through that sacrifice He brought redemption to the world of sin and death.

There are times when we must accept suffering humbly. It helps in our own purification and, if we are worthy enough, perhaps it may be used in some vicarious way for the good of the world. The realisation of the meaning of suffering, following that of the Loving Shepherd, was one of the greatest blessings that Green Pastures could bestow.

CHAPTER 7

Corroborative Evidence

Love never counts how much it gives
*   Nor yet the cost!*
So generous in thought and deed
*   It does not rest*
*   Till from its treasure store*
*   It brings forth happiness*
*   For those whom it would bless.*
As in the past, so more and more
Love still shall strive
*   To choose—and give—*
*   And ever give—the best.*

Ellen Hainsworth

SOME PEOPLE raise their eyebrows when spiritual healing is mentioned. "That's what cranks believe in," they say, but Green Pastures is a living proof that health can in so many instances be restored. An amazing variety of people have been helped to achieve freedom from worry and tension, fresh courage and health; for these and other blessings some of our guests return again and again. One guest found crying said that she had never been so happy in her life before, and explained that her tears were tears of gratitude. Afterwards she wrote, "I came to Green Pastures in great need of bodily rest and spiritual rebirth. I found both. The friendliness of the guests and staff, and the peacefulness of the garden refreshed my tired body. I also thank God for the Chapel where I was spiritually recreated. Green Pastures really became 'home' to me."

Many come after a crisis in life almost too much to bear. A widow looked a picture of misery as she passed through our doorway. She had lost husband and children in a motor accident, and the ultimate result had caused her such financial embarrassment that she feared she would lose her little home. She had lost faith in the goodness of God and was doubting His existence. We gave her all the love we could. Slowly she began to absorb the atmosphere and to attend the daily service. She was still unable to talk to anyone, and would sit at the back of the Chapel and hide herself away immediately afterwards. We all thanked God when the ice began to melt, but it was a very slow progress. One day she approached me to express gratitude for the help received, and from that time we were able to talk together. Her life still looked very barren, but she was beginning to accept it. Later she began to go out and enjoy the beauties of sea and countryside. By the time she left, while she would never forget her terrible tragedy, she was able to bear it courageously and nobly.

Another widow, again on the verge of a nervous breakdown, received such healing during a Healing service taken by the chaplain that she "knew" what she had to do with her life, and went back into the world to help others.

One man had suffered from asthma for years. Within days of his arrival he had considerable relief, and when he left, the malady had completely gone never to return; he wrote to say that he had given a thousand thanks to the Healing Shepherd for blessings received.

There was a lady with arthritis who arrived in a

wheel-chair in which she had been confined for years. With the new atmosphere around her she got up from her chair, and before leaving had walked the considerable distance to the sea. She returned home to care for those in need, and took two elderly women into her home.

Although Green Pastures is not a nursing home we accepted friends needing special nursing, who brought someone to help or had visits from a nurse. One who had what was said to be a terminal illness longed for our atmosphere of love, and was able to pay for a special nurse. She had a large ground-floor room with French windows, and on sunny days we were able to move her near to the garden. She was in constant pain, but was generally smiling. It was indeed a privilege to step down into the dark valley of suffering with her, and to help her radiant personality overcome the worn-out body. When she passed over we had a service of Thanksgiving for her life and witness.

With another invalid the problem was completely different. I was appalled when I saw the difficulty with which the Red Cross officials got her out of the ambulance, as she could not move at all. I told the attendant that we did not have facilities for dealing with such a case, but they said they could not take her back. The friend she had brought to help her was also an invalid, with no intention of sharing the duties. I discovered that the patient had come from a Home for the severely disabled, and was considered a three-nurse case. She pleaded to be allowed to stay as she had been longing to get away from the small hospital ward which she had shared with others for so long. It was easy to understand this. Her body was in a very broken condition but she had a lively and active mind. With considerable difficulty we managed to look after her, and she left much refreshed in mind to face again the monotony of the hospital ward. I often thought about her and prayed for her continuing courage and patience.

Another patient had been brought up in a Children's Home and had been put into service as soon as she was old enough. She had some physical problems, but I was asked to let her do light duties and try her out, for she had been drifting from job to job and had no family home. She was very slow and not very efficient, but she did adapt to our family life and became useful. We were surprised to find that she had a boy friend, whom she later married. She now has a full and enjoyable family life of her own, with a child who found happiness in the background she provided. Our doctor said that all the hard work put into the Home had been worthwhile if only for this one ray of sunshine.

We did not take permanent guests, but one very handicapped patient always seemed to "hang on". The only alternative for her was a Home for the disabled. I remembered the fate which the doctors had prescribed for me and how I had fought against it, so each year some odd job would be found for her. She would sit by the kitchen sink, crutches by her side, preparing vegetables, and telling an endless string of highly amusing anecdotes. During the afternoon she would take the telephone calls so that others could have a much needed break. She was a living proof that with a little help the mind and spirit can carry a troublesome body through many difficulties.

A patient who came straight from hospital with a rather disturbing prognosis slowly regained health, and when she returned home she wrote, "The last nine months have been the most difficult of my life. I could not understand why this should have happened to me, but in your Home I was spiritually reborn. Indeed, I feel I was never truly converted before. Now I walk in the Wondrous Light and have such a deep sense of joy and peace. I thank the Good Shepherd for the love and help I received. I was given the courage to start afresh and I thank Him for the wonderful work you are doing."

A retired missionary from hospital had worked so hard for others all her life that she had had a severe stroke. She was speechless and almost helpless, but by sheer willpower she learned to write again, aided by Vera, whose patience worked wonders. It is easy to appreciate the agony of this highly educated woman learning to copy letters as a young child does. We obtained a zimmer, and she managed a few hesitant steps. Her speech began to return and her writing improved. She went to a Home for Retired Missionaries and was able slowly to look after herself.

How grateful were those who sought some blessing, and then appeared to be fully healed! One mastoid sufferer came to us to gain strength to face a severe operation. She was in great pain, and we felt quite inadequate to help her. But as we prayed, the pain lessened, and when she returned home and visited the surgeon, to his amazement he pronounced her completely healed.

It was always an honour to have ministers and clergy, and very stimulating to be able to serve them. One was in a very distressed condition. He was in his early fifties and had a strong sense of vocation, but his doctor had told him that he should not continue working. It was very difficult for him to accept that his service for his Lord was over. His wife had strongly pressed him to come to Green Pastures but he was very reluctant, having come to the stage where he felt nothing was worthwhile. After a time I asked him if he would take a service, but he recoiled in horror and anguish: "My doctor says I shall never take a service again," he said, so the only course we could adopt was a concerted prayer therapy on his behalf. A sheer miracle happened at the next Healing service. He was completely transformed, and was convinced of his full healing. His doctor was amazed at the change in him, and gave him permission to return to part-time work. Shortly afterwards he was again working at full pressure for His Lord, and continued to do so until his normal retirement.

Another minister had an acute eye condition which prevented him from continuing his church duties. It was evident that he was facing a future without the work he loved so much. During his stay the Loving Shepherd touched his eyes and they were healed. He publicly gave thanks for this blessing.

One night I was awakened by the telephone. The caller was a complete stranger. She asked if I would join in a band of prayer, which I did. The vicar of her parish was fatally ill but felt that there was something he still had to do. The caller had had a great urge to promote prayers of intercession for him. Later I

58

heard that at that time her vicar was in a state of coma, the last sacrament had been given, and they were waiting for the end. Three hours later there was a dramatic change; he recovered from the coma and was sitting up drinking a cup of tea. Within a few days he had recovered sufficiently to leave the hospital and complete the mission he had to finish. The "Intercessors" roughly made a circle round the hospital—so that he was encircled by prayer that night.

Many other stories could be told of the wonderful power of the Healing Shepherd. We had abundant proof of His wonder-working Love but there were times when nothing seemed to happen, or the recipient held aloof. At such times we prayed to learn more of His will for the work of the Home, to be purer channels, and by His help receive a larger vision. We continued to serve Him as steadfastly as we were able, and to give Him the glory.

CHAPTER 8

Guidance Through The Years

The Lord will be your guide continually, and will satisfy your needs . . . He will give you strength.
                                        Isaiah 58.11 N.E.B.

A S GREEN Pastures became widely known, sufferers of a different type grew more prevalent. The conditions of the world and the tragedy of war and suffering became too much for them to bear; strain became intolerable, and psychological and emotional tensions resulted in a complete lack of faith, if it ever was there. There could be a deep sense of guilt, fear or unfulfilment which can bring on acute illnesses. Drugs and other medical means in many instances act only as pacifiers. So a complete and reasoned reappraisal of the gift of life is necessary to help those in such desperate need.

Many were on the point of suicide. One man considered his life was over. For many years he had run a successful business, but had failed and became bankrupt. After thirty years he came to us without money or friends. He found it all very difficult to understand, and was hurt because his so-called friends had abandoned him. His pride would not allow him to accept his new and humble position. One night he attempted suicide, and it was only by the Grace of God that we were able to save him, though he continued drinking whenever he could, sleeping and eating very little. Eventually the tragedy of his life was unfolded: invalided out of the army at nineteen with severe shell shock; eighteen months spent in a nerve hospital; his wife was a dominant woman. They had two daughters, and when he was discharged she exclaimed, "I'm sick of you. I can't stand this life any longer, and I'm taking the two girls with me." Not only did he lose his wife and daughters when he most needed them, but she also poisoned their minds against him. He began to drink, and his life was an increasing nightmare. We tried hard to relieve him of his chronic sense of failure and to restore him to a life that was worthwhile. Gradually his tension grew less and he slept better. Even his sleeping pills were handed over when the situation was passed. When he left he wrote, "I have got another job; I have no desire to drink any more, and I have not taken a sleeping pill for a fortnight. I go for long walks, and am able to enjoy so many things again. There is now a purpose in my life and I thank God for Green Pastures, where it was revealed to me."

One mentally ill woman was very suicidal. Her stay was temporary while her doctor arranged for her admittance to a mental hospital. He made it very clear that she was not to be left alone for one moment. Her husband was taking the night watch, and left her for two minutes. On his return he discovered that she had escaped through the open window, though she was on the first floor. She was clad in a flimsy nightdress and there was snow on the ground. We searched for over an hour in the dark and finally found her crouching in terror, blue with cold, under some trees. We did all we could to calm her; the next morning she was taken to a mental hospital. Her stay there was a long one, but she eventually went home to lead a normal life.

Sometimes I would unwittingly become involved with the most intimate problems of married life. One woman who had stayed with us discussed with the utmost frankness her most intimate problems. I realised that I was totally unable to help her materially but I could offer prayer. There was a very long period of outpouring during which I felt completely inadequate. Then she broke off in an exhausted fashion. I was prompted from within to say something very short and simple—which I could not remember afterwards. The Holy Spirit must have spoken through me, for to my astonishment she said, "Bless you. Your advice was just what I needed; I can now go back and deal with the problem!" Writing later, with grateful thanks, she said that her married life was now completely happy. I have never understood what happened, but God dealt with the situation.

In so many cases, "caring" was the essential ingredient for recovery. We learned that the nearer we got to the Good Shepherd the more valuable our help was. Scores of letters testified that healing had come; and in most of them there is a note of happy gratitude which recalls some lines from a well loved hymn:

"I came to Jesus as I was, weary and worn, and sad; I found in Him a resting place, and He has made me glad."

CHAPTER 9

Links In The Chain

*The Beauty of My Kingdom is its growth. In that
Kingdom there is always progress, a going on from
strength to strength, from Glory to Glory.*

"God Calling"

THROUGH SEVERAL YEARS the London Executive,
with Dr. A. D. Beldon, D.D. and Mr. Griffith
Evans, F.R.C.S., M.A., D.M., as Co-Chairmen, met
regularly, with frequent visits to Green Pastures for
the special functions which seemed to come up so
quickly. I can never say how much Green Pastures
owes to those pioneers, and I thank the Good
Shepherd for their love and wisdom that encouraged
me to go forward.

We also gathered round us a band of interested
local people, who formed the Local Advisory Committee that helped so generously with summer fetes,
coffee mornings, and in so many other ways.

The Rev. Nigel Porter, B.A., was our first President
and a tower of strength. In one speech he referred to
a woman who said, "Not only have I regained my
strength at Green Pastures, but my reason was also
saved." Her husband's death had broken her but her
stay enabled her to lead a life of self-sacrifice for
others.

The Rev. Ian Hope, our first Chaplain, said, "It is
good to see the healing process going on during the
time our guests have been in the Home, and to have

later news telling of the help received. These testimonies are perhaps the most effective and encouraging witness to the reality of the power of God."

Quotations from other Chaplains: "Many have derived great spiritual and physical benefit from the calm and prayerful atmosphere prevailing," wrote the Rev. A. Dewhurst. "There is great need for this kind of Christian witness, and I pray that God will continue to bless the Home."

The Rev. K. J. Hibberd: "How rewarding the work became! As it grew in volume one had the sense of being carried along by the Holy Spirit, in what I believe to be a splendid piece of spiritual pioneering adventure . . . A great deal of the work can be seen to bear fruit, but a great deal more, equally fruitful, will remain untold."

The Rev. D. H. Cummings, B.A.: "I can say with all sincerity that I became thoroughly convinced of the real value of Green Pastures in helping to meet the needs of people for spiritual and divine healing. Guests would spontaneously testify when talking to me to the way in which they had been helped."

Pastor Bernard Dawson: "I hope that the continuing deep joy and peace of the Home, together with God's wonderful blessing, may continue to abide with you."

The Home can never adequately express its gratitude for the wonderful honorary services given by our doctors—Kenneth and Frances McAll, R. V. Garrett, Ph.D.; and our solicitors—John I. Miller and J. Grange-Bennett, M.A., and others too numerous to mention, one of whom said, "Green Pastures is of great importance, for it is the place where prayer provides the Powerhouse through which the Love of the Good Shepherd can function; where Vision becomes reality; and new life flows out to the needy."

So many cases came straight from hospital, or were elderly, and needed more permanent accommodation, so the London Executive met the new challenge and were guided to buy a nearby house for the necessary expansion. Thus was founded "Still Waters", which catered for about eighteen guests. Although the house was sold later, it rendered valuable service as a further link in the chain.

When the Good Shepherd plans some great thing for the future He is careful to make precise preparations. As the Plan emerges and we begin to understand the vision, we see the importance of the many links in the chain which, in Divine Providence, are so essential.

There were periods during my happy service at Green Pastures when I found it difficult to carry out a full and active life, and often I was forced to spend my off-duty days in bed; perhaps I was still considered by some to be an invalid. As the years passed it became more difficult to cope with the ever-increasing demands of the Home. I suggested to the London Executive that probably the time had come when another Warden should be appointed, thinking there was now adequate scope for a married Minister and wife. The Executive agreed, and we were in the midst of these arrangements when the untimely deaths of Dr. Belden, Mr. Griffith Evans and two other members of the Executive, changed all the plans, and the Local Advisory Committee, with some additional members, took on Executive status.

This new Committee continued the search for another Warden, but thought in terms of another woman rather than a married couple, and they then informed me they had very reluctantly decided that my health was no longer robust enough to allow me to continue as Warden.

I was slow to realise the full implications of this inevitable decision; I was deeply troubled; I was rebellious, for my greatest longing was to continue in the active Healing Ministry. As I accepted the decision I realised that I was only a link and that the whole chain was to be forged for His Glory.

Another link was provided by Mrs. Iris Delaselle, who took on the onerous duties of the Wardenship, bringing to the Home another facet of service with her various skills and capabilities; she was helped by Miss Eva Martin, who for several years had been the Secretary, and who continued to fulfil her valuable duties.

Yet another link was provided by the Rev. Lewis MacLachlan, and his wife, who had served in the China Mission Field. He was a Master of Arts, and his literary ability had been acknowledged by Christians through his books on prayer and healing. He was, therefore, ideally fitted to play a vital role in the development of Green Pastures. His wife, with her Scots practicality, brought a great measure of common sense to the work.

But there was another linch pin required if the chain were to gather in strength and stay the course, and the vision continue to be achieved. This valuable addition was provided by the Good Shepherd in the person of the Rev. William E. Burridge. I first met him when he had just begun his ministry in the Bournemouth area. He had accepted an invitation to attend a Conference on Healing, and during one of the intervals I was able to tell him about the Home. He was enthusiastic and interested, and later gladly agreed to join the Local Advisory Committee.

I was still to learn from him that God had sought him out to prepare him for work in the field of Divine Healing, when he was serving as Methodist Minister in Guernsey. He had been shown by God the poverty of his own prayer life, and the result was his need to share with others. He plunged into the formation of a School of Prayer, but he could not cope with the severe programme he had set himself. There followed a painful reaction in his body, and recurrence of a malady that had dogged his life as a theological student. His Ministry became clouded, for he was sick with pain. He was faced with an enigma, for the purpose of the School, which was very successful, was to teach the significance of prayer, and to bring Jesus-wholeness to those attending; but to him, the teacher, it brought just the opposite! In the past he had also suffered from a debilitating nervous complaint and that also returned with new intensity.

He awoke one morning with the most agonising pain in the abdomen; the agony was so great that he collapsed on the bedroom floor with a cry of despair. His wife had been awakened by the commotion, and was, of course, concerned by his condition. She at once became the instrument of the Lord, and fired an arrow of retort which was to hit its mark and start a healing chain of events. "Why don't you practise what you preach?" she exclaimed. This retort pierced and quickened him. It was indeed the solution and in kneeling prayer a new commitment to his Lord was made. The immediate response was that a healing balm of love flowed through him and he was healed in a second. God had brought him to a new under-standing of the Healing Ministry and the power of believing prayer. He felt that he was now committed to a new dimension of his Ministry, but he was not to preach it in Guernsey, for such are the vicissitudes of a Methodist minister's life that he is "here to-day and elsewhere to-morrow". He was guided to Bourne-mouth and it so happened that the very first letter that he opened upon arrival led to his meeting with us. God certainly wasted no time!

I invited him to visit Green Pastures and he was captivated by its atmosphere of serenity and love. I was delighted that he fully realised the immense importance of this work in the life of the Church and that he was fully committed to a Ministry of Healing, his vision embracing the existence of such a Home.

His presence on our committee was reinforced by swift incursions into the Crowhurst fellowship, and his enthusiasm gave a great boost to the work of our Home. He was asked to become the new Director, and the Methodist Conference agreed to second him to take up the appointment.

With his appointment the Home was ready to take another great step forward. Green Pastures had to be enlarged again, and the building programme, as originally envisaged, completed. It was the only way in which it could endeavour to meet the growing demands of an increasingly materialistic and God-denying country.

But where was the money to come from? While the Home was not making a loss its purpose discounted the making of sufficient profit to finance a building scheme of such magnitude. The existing premises had now been used for well over a decade and badly needed a facelift, and the committee were faced with providing the adequate premises in which a caring and teaching Ministry could be fulfilled. I prayed that those who now had to decide the policy would be led to adopt a bold policy which was consistent with the faith of the past. And they were led.

In 1971 the Executive, under the Directorship of the Rev. W. Burridge, decided to go ahead with the re-building—additional bedrooms, a new dining room and office, and a new Chapel.

The Chapel had for so long been the hub of our activities, but it was too small. I was present on the site when it was demolished and a great sadness came over me.

The building work was finally completed, a very attractive and modern structure, and I praised God that I was able to be present at the re-dedication of His work.

Returning to my own home that day I rejoiced at the way in which the Good Shepherd had not only guided us from the beginning, leading us along the path of understanding, but had also provided successors with vision and courage, so that His work could develop and increase. The pattern of things was at last more clear to me.

CHAPTER 10

The Fruits of Guidance

*The tender compassion of our God . . . will rise
upon us . . . to guide our feet into the way of peace.*
Luke I.78-79. N.E.B.

THIS BOOK TELLS very simply how God commissions and empowers His servants to go forward in the way He would have them travel.

We were privileged through the years to have an ever-deepening experience of seeing the Good Shepherd's Healing Ministry. The Home has travelled a long road since my humble beginnings, but the fundamental truths remain the same. There are multitudes to-day who have lost their faith and are immersed in a pagan, permissive society. Medical researchers confirm that there is evidence of increasing mental and nervous disorders and that the Home should be geared to give all who enter its doors a greater renewal of strength to cope with the ever-growing problems of life as it will be lived in the later years of this century.

The power of the Holy Spirit is available for Green Pastures to fulfil its divine purpose. The guests can realise His Presence and Healing Love, for at the centre there is—and always will be—the Lord Jesus Himself, the Master Healer; the Home is simply a channel. It could not exist without the Church, for it is an extension of the Church's work, and the Church needs such Homes to show the love of the Great

Shepherd in action. One of the most significant events of the first half of this century has been the rediscovery of the Healing Ministry. The second half should reveal and acknowledge more than ever the necessity for Homes like Green Pastures and other havens for body and soul.

Much emphasis today is on "remedial" work, which is necessary, but the Shepherd is available not only to those who have fallen physically or mentally, but also to close the gap between God's Kingdom and the "Permissive Society". As the gap grows wider, the need for preventive medicine will become more important.

Many schools have become secular, with very little Christian faith taught. Their accent is on the mechanics of the body and the materialistic outlook, but the Church must put the emphasis upon the "wholeness" of life, involving hygiene of body, mind and spirit. There is a tremendous field to be explored here. Young people and married couples have many problems to face; the responsibilities of parenthood are frequently undertaken very lightly, with the expectation that the State will provide all necessities. If Green Pastures can show that the Christian family with its love and willing acceptance of responsibility is still a most rewarding and satisfying experience, it will have fulfilled a valuable task, for Jesus came to offer abundant life to all.

There is a particularly onerous road for clergy, ministers, doctors and welfare workers, and where better to receive spiritual refreshment than at Green Pastures and similar Homes in the company of others treading the same path of dedication?

Now, in my retirement, with my life span nearly completed, I look back in the deepest awe, for we had only a slight glimpse of the Plan of the Great Shepherd, and it seems incredible that He should take and use such frail and faulty instruments as channels for His Love and Healing Power. The threads for this work are drawn from the infinite past; they stretch forth into the far distant future; they have touched—and will touch—many lives with peace and health and beauty. Treasures of great wealth there are—kindly deeds done, the joys of fellowship and service and sacrifice, growing to fruition in other lives in the days to come.

> "Praise, my soul, the King of Heaven:
>   To His feet thy tribute bring,
> Ransomed, healed, restored, forgiven—
>   Who like thee His praise should sing?"

Epilogue

By the Rev. William Burridge
(Director and Chaplain of Green Pastures)

TO CONTRIBUTE this Epilogue to Sister Ruth Hainsworth's impressive story is a great privilege, enabling me as it does to report on further developments at Green Pastures that she so courageously founded in the faith we share that God, in His omnipotent love, will continue to lead and guide us.

Our obligations are increasing rapidly and the scope is widening. During the past months eager parties have come from Germany, Sweden and Finland to learn of the manifold ways in which the Healing Christ works. Individuals from America, Canada, Australia, Denmark, Peru, Liberia, Bolivia and other far places have arrived to experience an ever-deepening awareness of the Christ who is both cosmic and redeeming, and among them we have noticed a firm desire to establish similar Homes of Healing in their respective lands.

The physical shape of the Home continues to expand as it becomes obvious that the diversity of man's needs must be met by a diversity of facilities. For many who are sick *rest* is most essential but for others *activity* is of paramount importance; so in addition to the basic practices of prayer, worship and counselling we are adding the therapeutic activities of crafts, art and creative writing. We hope to build later an occupational therapy room and an outdoor heated swimming pool, and to introduce other leisure facilities for those able to take advantage of them as they recover wholeness.

I need not continue the history of the healings occurring at the Home but one particularly stands out in my memory as an example of the effect of love and prayer and their influence by the Holy Spirit. A victim of Anorexia Nervosa (a terribly wasting disease), Rosemary came to us looking like a starving refugee from a concentration camp. (Is it any wonder that our hearts sometimes fail in the presence of such frightening sickness?) But a wonderful and complete healing was brought about by the grace of God; and since then she has entered a most demanding profession, completed a year's service without sick leave, and become a beautiful figure on skis; and her first real holiday in Austria was therefore a celebration of joyful gratitude.

We continually praise God for the 1972 expansion and modernisation. When contemplated on my arrival at Green Pastures as the new Director and Chaplain the task seemed insurmountable at a cost of £80,000! But once again God's bounty, which we erringly felt to be limited in spite of His ever-recurring promise, proved to be all-sufficient, and our faith was strengthened and renewed. Most of us find that faith does call for renewal from time to time, for we are but human and subject to human frailties. We ought continually to bear in mind that "All things are possible" to Him as His resources are infinite. Green Pastures was founded on this Truth and it has brought together in love Methodists, Baptists, Anglicans, Pentecostalists, Roman Catholics and others of differing creeds, an unthinkable achievement not so many years ago. Is not that too a miracle?

In conclusion we ask for the daily prayers of all who read this remarkable book that we may be supported in faith that "the best is yet to be"—*and it will be.*

W.B.